START Reading

Sea Creatures

Anne Faundez

QED Publishing

First published in the UK in 2004 by
QED Publishing
A division of Quarto Publishing plc
The Fitzpatrick Building
188–194 York Way, London N7 9QP

A Catalogue record for this book is available from the British Library.

ISBN 1 84538 009 6

Written by Anne Faundez
Designed by Zeta Jones
Editor Hannah Ray
Picture Researcher Joanne Beardwell

Series Consultant Anne Faundez
Creative Director Louise Morley
Editorial Manager Jean Coppendale

Printed and bound in China

Picture credits

Key: t = top, b = bottom, m = middle, c = centre, l = left, r = right

Contents

Under the sea

Lots of amazing creatures live in the sea. Some are large and some are small.

Some live deep in the ocean and some live along the shore.

The sea is home to animals of all sorts of different colours, shapes, sizes and patterns.

Manatees

Manatees are **mammals**. They cannot breathe underwater and come up to the surface for air.

They use their flippers to crawl along the seabed.

6

Manatees talk to each other, or **communicate**, by squealing.

They are gentle creatures and like to play. They even kiss each other.

Octopuses

Octopuses have eight long arms called tentacles. These are covered in suckers.

Octopuses use their tentacles to grip onto rocks and other surfaces. They also use their tentacles to catch food.

When attacked, octopuses shoot black ink at their enemies.

Octopuses can also hide by changing their skin colour to match their surroundings. This is called **camouflage**.

Seahorses

Seahorses are small creatures that are a type of fish. Some seahorses are only 5cm long.

Seahorses swim along using fins on their backs to help them to move forwards.

The female lays her eggs in the male's pouch, which is like a small bag. The eggs stay in the pouch until they are ready to **hatch**.

Barracudas

Barracudas live in warm seas. Their long, or **streamlined**, body helps them to move fast in search of **prey**.

They have strong jaws and lots of sharp teeth. They are **carnivores** and eat smaller fish. They have even been known to attack humans.

13

Angelfish

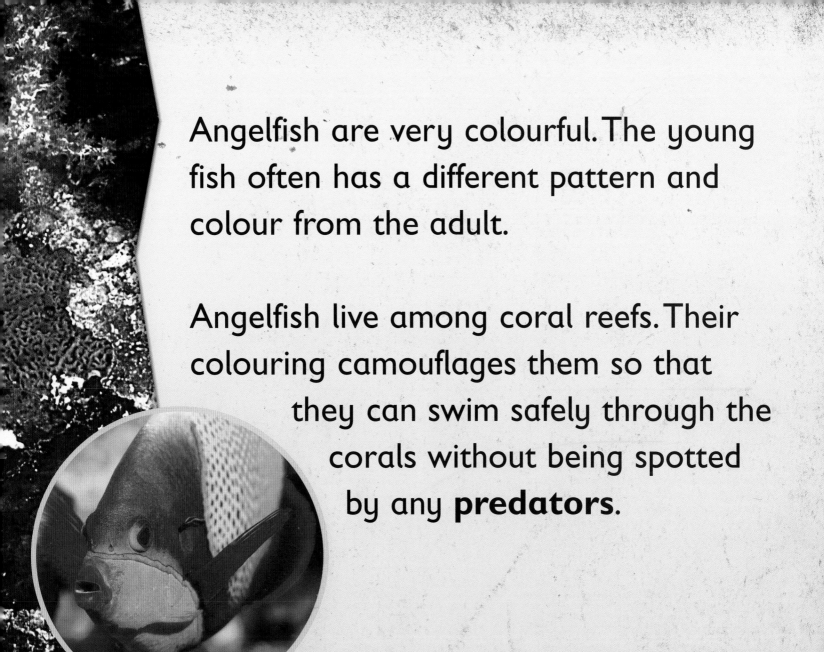

Angelfish are very colourful. The young fish often has a different pattern and colour from the adult.

Angelfish live among coral reefs. Their colouring camouflages them so that they can swim safely through the corals without being spotted by any **predators**.

Seals

Seals look clumsy on land, but they are good swimmers and move very fast through water.

A layer of fat, called blubber, keeps the seals warm in cold seas.

Baby seals, or pups, are very playful.

Sea anemones

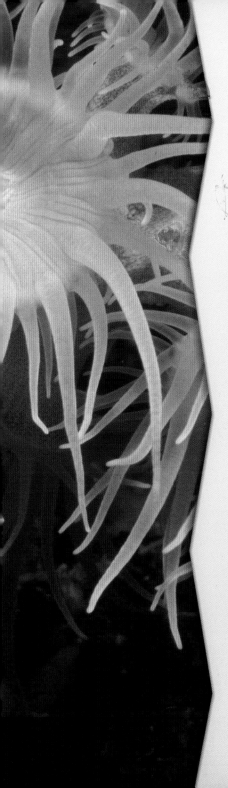

Sea anemones look like plants, but they are a type of animal.

They are brightly coloured with long, wavy tentacles. They have a mouth in the middle of their bodies.

Sea anemones attach themselves to corals and rocks, and use their tentacles to catch their prey.

Sea anemones are carnivores and eat small fish, shrimps and crabs.

Sharks

Sharks are fierce predators and eat other sea animals.

They swim in the open sea as well as along coasts and reefs.

Sharks have huge, strong jaws and several rows of sharp teeth. If they lose a tooth, another one quickly grows in its place.

camouflage – something that makes an animal look part of its surroundings.

carnivore – an animal that eats other animals.

communicate – a way of 'talking' among animals.

hatch – when an animal breaks out of the egg.

mammals – an animal that feeds on its mother's milk.

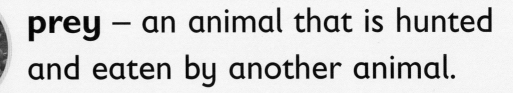

prey – an animal that is hunted and eaten by another animal.

predator – an animal that hunts, kills and eats other animals.

streamlined – a body that is long and thin and can move quickly.

Index

Carers' and teachers' notes

- Look at the front cover. Ask your child what he/she can see? What might the book be about?
- Point out the title and read it to your child. Identify the author's name. Explain that the word 'author' means the person who wrote the book.
- Look at the back cover. What does it say? Does it make your child want to read the book?
- Find the contents, the index and the glossary. Explain that this book gives facts and information (i.e. it is non-fiction), rather than telling a story (fiction).
- Ask your child to look out for the words in **bold** type. Each time he/she spots one, look it up in the glossary. Explain that the glossary helps us to understand difficult or unusual words.
- Flick through the book. Which pages does your child like the best? Which would he/she like to read first? Explain that the book does not have to be read from beginning to end, but can be dipped into.

- Count the animals on each page. What colours are they? Do they have flippers, fins or tentacles?
- Is your child familiar with any of the sea creatures? Has he/she seen the creatures in real life? Where did he/she see them? Are there any of the creatures that your child would like to see?
- Read about octopuses on page 9. How many tentacles does an octopus have? Can your child pretend to be an octopus? How would an octopus move?
- Use the contents page to find the entry for seals. Ask the child to draw a seal. Together, think of a sentence about the seal. Write the sentence for your child, underneath the picture.
- Which animal looks like a plant?
- Look back through the photos in the book. Can your child remember the names of the animals? Which is his/her favourite?